# The Vietnam War

## *THE BEST ONE-HOUR HISTORY*

Robert Freeman

The Best One-Hour History™

Kendall Lane Publishers, Palo Alto, CA

Copyright © 2013, Robert Freeman

ISBN-13: 978-0-9892502-8-3

*The author gratefully acknowledges the generous help of Peter Maslowski who read and improved upon several iterations of the text. Without his contribution this would be a much lesser book.*

# Contents

# Southeast Asia

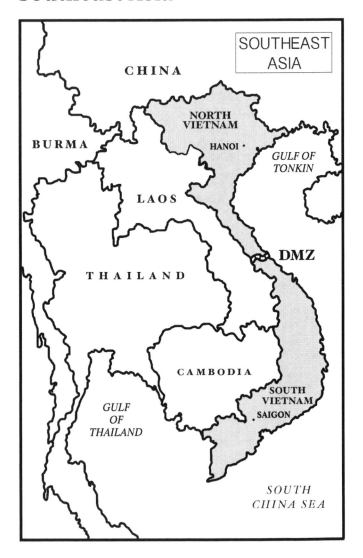

# 1 Introduction

The Vietnam War was the longest war in U.S. history up to that time. It was a battle between the richest country in the world and one of the poorest, between the most powerful industrialized nation on earth and a feudal society that had not even entered the industrial age. It cost the U.S. over $450 billion, wrecked the American economy, grievously damaged U.S. prestige in the world, and resulted in the deaths of over 58,000 Americans. It also resulted in the direct deaths of an estimated 3 million southeast Asians. It divided the U.S. as no event since the Civil War ever had. It was the first war that America ever lost.

The War grew out of a bedevilingly complex mixture of colonialism, nationalism, anti-communism and a civil war much like America's that pitted a secessionist south against a unifying north. Its occurrence, from the late 1940s to the mid-1970s, spanned the most dangerous years of the Cold War. Its major tensions almost perfectly mirrored the essential tensions of the Cold War. And precisely because of this, it proved impossible for the U.S. to stay out of Vietnam. But for reasons we shall see below, it also proved impossible for the U.S. to win. This was the fundamental source of the "quagmire" and the tragedy of Vietnam: the U.S. couldn't stay out; but it could never manage to win.

This book traces the War's origin in the crucible of the Cold War, through its escalation in the 1960s, and its ending in the mid-1970s. It explores some of the major themes that defined the War. Then, it examines in some detail why the U.S. lost the War and the cost of that loss to the American self-image. Finally, it presents a timeline of major occurrences and turning points during the War.

# 2 Stages of the War

The Vietnam War evolved through five distinct stages. It began as a colonial matter in the aftermath of World War II. Then, when the French left in 1956, there was a period in which the U.S. became entrapped by its own rigid commitment to anti-communism. The U.S. began fighting the War directly in 1965, but began to reverse that policy, drawing down its troops, in 1969. Finally, in 1973 the U.S. withdrew its forces altogether, handing the fighting over to the Republic of (South) Vietnam. The Republic of Vietnam collapsed in 1975 under an invasion by the North. Following, are expanded descriptions of each of these stages.

## 1945 – 1954: Colonial Legacy and Anti-Communist Context

The roots of America's involvement in Vietnam date to the closing days of World War II. Developing countries around the globe began fighting wars for national liberation—trying to throw off the yoke of colonial domination by Western powers. In this context, four separate but closely intertwined threads emerged to define the essential impetus for the War: anti-colonialism; the post-War U.S. policy of "containment"; the communist takeover of China in 1949; and the McCarthy-led anti-communist witch-hunts of the early 1950s.

*Colonial Origins.* Vietnam had fought foreign domination—by the Chinese, the French, the Japanese, and again by the French—for hundreds of years. From the 1860s until World War II, the French dominated Southeast Asia in an area called French Indochina. It included what today is known as Vietnam, Laos, and Cambodia. During World War II, the Japanese took over by defeating the French occupiers. This dealt a fatal blow to the reputation of the French in the eyes of the Vietnamese. But after Japan surrendered to the U.S. in 1945, France returned and re-occupied Vietnam.

In 1946, Vietnam appealed to President Truman for help in liberating itself from French re-occupation. But the U.S. rebuffed Vietnam's request for help. When the situation escalated into a war between Vietnamese nationalists and the French, the U.S. helped the French, providing them with military advisers and money. The first U.S. military advisers arrived in Vietnam in 1950. By 1953, the U.S. was paying 80% of France's costs of running the War.

Ironically, the Vietnamese had fashioned their war for independence after the U.S.'s own Revolutionary

War, even quoting Thomas Jefferson in the opening words of their own Declaration of Independence: "All men are created equal. They are endowed by their Creator with certain inalienable rights. Among these are Life, Liberty and the pursuit of Happiness." But Ho Chi Minh, Vietnam's leader, though first and foremost a nationalist, was also a communist. Because of this, the U.S. wanted nothing to do with him. The U.S.'s rejection of Ho's request for assistance and its support of the French instead, drove the Vietnamese even further into the communist camp.

It turned first to China and later to the Soviet Union for help in evicting the foreign occupiers. Vietnam viewed the U.S.'s support for France's re-occupation as a bitter betrayal, one it would never forget. That would make it impossible for the U.S. to ever win the hearts and minds of the Vietnamese people. Without such support, it would make it all but impossible for the U.S. to win the War. Thus, from its earliest beginnings, the ultimate course of the War had been set.

*The Containment Context.* The U.S. justified its support of the French by its policy of Containment. This doctrine, formulated by George Kennan of the State Department in 1946, held that the U.S. should prevent the Soviet Union from expanding beyond its existing area of influence. To win World War II, the Soviet Union had marched through Eastern Europe on the way to Berlin. It took control of over 150,000 square miles of territory including Poland, Czechoslovakia,

Romania, Bulgaria, and Hungary. Stalin declared at Yalta, in February 1945, that he was not going to give up this territory. The U.S. was intent that the Soviets should not expand into Asia as well, and vowed to "contain" them to their then-current borders.

The Korean War, from 1950 to 1953, was the first "hot" test of this policy. But that war was fought to a standstill and never won. The U.S. viewed Vietnam as another effort at communist expansion. In this context, President Eisenhower spoke of "dominoes" that might fall should the U.S. allow even one country in Southeast Asia to "go communist." The worst scenario had the dominoes falling into Cambodia and Laos, through Thailand and Burma and all the way to India. All of Asia would be lost! In 1961, the CIA repudiated the "domino theory" but by then the U.S. was committed to the War and would continue it for yet another 12 years.

*Communist Takeover of China.* U.S. desperation to contain communism was dealt a grievous setback in 1949 when the pro-U.S. government of China fell to a communist insurgency. Since the 1920s, China had been embroiled in a civil war, between wealthy capitalist oligarchs and communists. The oligarchs, called Nationalists, were led by General Chaing Kai Shek. The communists were led by the revolutionary Mao Zedong. The U.S. had gone to great lengths to help the Nationalists defeat the communists. It had provided them with money, weapons, training, and logistical support. But the communists won.

The most populous country on earth had joined America's foremost enemy—the Soviet Union—in an ideological alliance that seemingly posed a profound threat to U.S. interests in the world. Much of Africa, assisted sometimes by Soviet support, was rebelling from a century of colonial domination by Western powers. India had attained independence from Britain in 1947 and had aligned itself with the Soviet Union. And now, most of Asia, save only for the southwest (what we today call the "Middle East"), found itself under communist rule or influence. Panic is not too strong a word to describe the mood in U.S. foreign policy circles toward communist activity in Vietnam.

*McCarthyism.* Finally, in the early 1950s, the U.S. went through a "witch-hunt," looking to rid the government of communists—especially officials from the Democratic Truman administration who had supposedly "lost China." Led by Republican U.S. Senator Joe McCarthy, it labeled broad swaths of American government officials as "communist sympathizers." The "Red Scare" as it was called became a vicious campaign to demonize political opponents. Many careers, both inside and outside the government, were ruined by rumors, innuendoes, and "black lists" of supposed "enemies of the state."

Once burned by McCarthyism, U.S. leaders vowed they would never again appear to be "soft on communism." This led them to pursue policies in Vietnam that they themselves deemed foolish.

It led them to stay with the War long after it had become obvious that it was unwinnable in any acceptable manner. Even Republicans felt it necessary to inoculate themselves from the charge of being soft on communism. The bombing campaign of the War reached its highest intensity under Republican president Richard Nixon.

In a very real sense, then, the "Red-baiting" of the 1950s made it all but inevitable that the U.S. would become mired in Vietnam in the 1960s. Despite hundreds of millions of dollars in U.S. assistance, the French were decisively defeated at the battle of Dien Bien Phu in May, 1954. Following a peace conference in Geneva, Switzerland, France left Vietnam. Fatefully, carrying the flag of anti-communism, the U.S. picked up where the French had left off.

## 1955 – 1964: Creeping Entrapment

Between 1955 and 1964, the U.S. became progressively mired in the conflict in Vietnam. Presidents Eisenhower, Kennedy and Johnson all faced the same insoluble challenge: they couldn't allow Vietnam to fall to the communists; but, after Korea, they didn't want to get involved in another land war in Asia, either. Their approaches to deal with this conundrum were all the same: provide enough support not to lose, but never quite enough to actually win. This was a formula for sustained frustration and "creeping entrapment."

In 1954 a conference was held in Geneva, Switzerland to decide the fate of Vietnam. It produced a set of Accords that included three important provisions:

- First, factions from the North (communist) and South (non-communist) would be separated by the 17th parallel. This was explicitly *not* a division of one country into two countries. Rather, it was a "regroupment" line behind which the French would regroup prior to their departure;

- Second, by 1956, nation-wide elections would be held, with the winner assuming control of a new national government; and

- Third, foreign countries would not increase their military forces in Vietnam.

All three of these provisions were quickly violated by the U.S. Following the conference, the U.S. installed a hand-picked leader in the south, Bao Dai. This former "emperor" of Vietnam had been the puppet of both the French and the Japanese during their colonial occupations of Indochina. His appointment as leader of the U.S.-supported faction poisoned the already jaundiced Vietnamese perceptions of U.S. motives.

Within a year, however, Boa Dai was replaced by Ngo Diem, a Vietnamese national who had been living in New Jersey. The U.S. pressured Diem to boycott the 1956 Geneva-sponsored elections and declare the "Republic of South Vietnam" a new, sovereign, and independent state. This creation of a separate state went directly against the Geneva Accords. It also went against the wishes of the Vietnamese people who overwhelmingly wanted national unity. Asked why the U.S. did not support the elections, President Eisenhower stated flatly, "our guys would have lost."

When Diem refused national elections, the War, in addition to already being about nationalism and communism, suddenly became a civil war as well, not unlike the U.S. Civil War. The North, under Ho Chi Minh, pursued national unification. The South, under Diem, fought for secession and the creation of an independent nation. In 1960, the government in the North helped nationalist rebels in the South organize an insurgency against the U.S.-installed Diem regime. They formed the National Liberation Front (NLF), later known as the Viet Cong. The Viet Cong were native to the south and so proved extremely difficult to eradicate.

By 1960, South Vietnam had become the largest recipient of U.S. economic aid in the world. Instability, however, continued to grow. There were two coup attempts that year against Diem, one by his own generals, the other by a group of right wing political leaders. Both were repulsed with the help of the U.S. but neither spoke well of Diem's ability to create a viable government. In 1961, fearful of losing Vietnam to the communists, President Kennedy began ratcheting up U.S. support.

He approved the use of advisers to the Army of the Republic of (South) Vietnam (ARVN) and authorized the use of napalm and chemical defoliants over thousands of square miles of forest, jungle and agricultural land. Kennedy began shipments of helicopters and troop transports to South Vietnam and provided U.S. pilots to fly ARVN soldiers into battle. When Kennedy entered office there had been 700 of these U.S. advisers in Vietnam. By 1962, there were over 12,000. Kennedy was well aware that all of these moves violated the Geneva Accords.

By late 1963, the U.S. had lost confidence in Diem. It prompted a group of generals to overthrow him. On November 1, he and his brother were killed in the back of an armored personnel carrier. But the coup inflamed the political atmosphere in Vietnam. Everyone knew the U.S. had been behind it and this undermined the legitimacy of the new government. Worse, the generals proved even less effective at governing than Diem had been. Over the next three years, seven different governments operated in South Vietnam.

This instability made it difficult to make progress in the War. Repeated regime changes left the government in a state of virtual anarchy. Into this vacuum, the Viet Cong launched major military offensives against the government. Students, workers and religious leaders took to the streets to protest the oppression that was used to keep order. This provoked still more repression. In early 1964,

American intelligence warned that the government could only survive for "a few weeks or months." The much-feared collapse of the first domino was within sight. A sense of desperation pervaded Washington. Something dramatic needed to be done.

In August 1964, a U.S. destroyer reported that on two separate occasions it was fired upon in the Gulf of Tonkin near the coast of North Vietnam. In response, and with virtually no debate, the U.S. Congress granted the president the authority to pursue war in Vietnam with whatever means and according to whatever judgment he deemed necessary. Only two senators voted against the Gulf of Tonkin Resolution, calling it a "pre-dated blank check for war."

While there was some confusion at the time about whether the U.S. ship was actually attacked, history would reveal that at least the second attack never occurred. It had been manufactured to give the U.S. a suitable *casus belli*—a justification for war. It was under authority of the Gulf of Tonkin Resolution that presidents Johnson and Nixon dramatically expanded the War over the next five years.

## 1965 – 1969: Escalation and Americanization

In early 1965, the U.S. changed strategy and initiated an entirely new phase of the War. While before, ARVN did the fighting with U.S. support, now U.S. forces would carry the brunt of the fighting themselves. In March, the U.S began sustained bombing of North Vietnam through a campaign called "Rolling Thunder." Later that year, it also began to deploy ground-based combat troops for the first time. The change was momentous. The commitment of U.S. troops and prestige would make it extraordinarily difficult for the U.S. to withdraw unless it had secured a clear-cut military/political victory. That would prove impossible to achieve.

In July 1965, the first huge wave of these new combat troops arrived. By the end of 1965, there were 185,000 U.S. troops in Vietnam. In 1966 the number jumped to 385,000, and to 462,000 by the end of 1967. By mid-1968, with over half a million U.S. soldiers in Vietnam, the U.S. commander, General William Westmoreland, was requesting an additional 206,000 troops. That request was denied. U.S. troop count crested at 538,000 in April of 1969.

The fighting in Vietnam was unlike anything the U.S. Army had ever trained for. It involved new terrain—jungles and rice paddies—not the familiar plains of Europe where U.S. military doctrine and strategy had been honed. It was a "People's War" that employed a complex and shifting mixture of subversion, terrorism, guerrilla warfare, and conventional warfare that baffled—and ultimately defeated—U.S. military leaders. Finally, the Viet Cong used local communities for support and cover. U.S. forces could not distinguish combatants from civilians. This resulted in hundreds of thousands of civilians being accidentally—and often intentionally—killed.

Free Fire Zones were created to deal with the fact that guerilla forces often used these local villages as staging areas for their attacks. In such Zones, anything that moved—men, women, children, farm animals—was subject to be killed. The rationale for this policy was that this was one of the few certain ways to eradicate Viet Cong and their supporters. Free Fire Zones led to the mentality expressed by one U.S. army major who was questioned about the intensity of the attack on a Mekong River Delta farming hamlet: "We had to destroy the village in order to save it." Such attitudes served more often than not to turn the civilian population against the U.S.

In addition to escalation of the ground war, the air war was expanded as well. In 1966, U.S. aircraft flew 139,000 sorties against targets in North Vietnam. They flew 58,000 sorties against targets in neutral Laos. In South Vietnam, where most of the War's fighting occurred, they flew 161,000 sorties. Besides bombs, the U.S. also sprayed much of Vietnam with defoliants, to remove the leaves from vegetation and deprive the enemy of hiding places. During the War, 21 million gallons of the defoliant Agent Orange were sprayed on Vietnam, destroying an estimated 50% of the country's forests and creating an environmental catastrophe. The active ingredient in Agent Orange, dioxin, is a known carcinogen and has passed down its effects to at least three generations of Vietnamese civilians. An estimated half a million American soldiers were exposed to Agent Orange in Vietnam.

The dramatic expansion in both the scale and the intensity of the War caused widespread collapse in Vietnamese society. In 1966, as a result of military operations, 785,000 peasants became refugees. By 1969, more than 10% of the entire peasant population of Vietnam had been uprooted from its ancestral homelands. The American style of warfare, with its reliance on massive destruction from the air and "Search and Destroy" operations on the ground served to undercut progress in the political sphere by destroying many of the country's cultural traditions, social structures, and economic systems. Paradoxically, therefore, it made it increasingly impossible to secure political peace.

It was not only the military part of the War that was "Americanized." The entire country experienced the invasion of an alien culture and people. Black markets sprung up in everything from cigarettes and beer to ammunition and automobiles. Monetary inflation distorted the prices of almost all goods. A massive economic gap opened up between those who supported the War—mainly politically-connected city-dwellers—and those who didn't—peasants in the countryside. Millions of peasants, uprooted from their homes, moved to the cities in search of work. Urban populations exploded. Many women were forced into prostitution. Amidst the social destruction, support for the War and its American sponsors plummeted. This made local populations easy prey for recruitment by the Viet Cong.

One of the premises of U.S. strategy was that the U.S. would be able to escalate the fighting to a point beyond which the North could not go. President Nixon's National Security Adviser, Henry Kissinger, expressed this in 1970, stating "A fourth rate power like North Vietnam must have a breaking point." In fact, North Vietnam, aided by China and the Soviet Union, matched U.S. escalation every year of the War. After the start of Rolling Thunder the entire country of North Vietnam was mobilized in support of the War.

By late 1967, the U.S. military command had convinced itself that it was winning the War. But in January 1968, during the annual Lunar New Year celebration, named "Tet," the North Vietnamese Army (NVA) and Viet Cong staged a series of simultaneous, nation-wide attacks on dozens of cities and U.S. military bases throughout South Vietnam. The attacks stunned the U.S., which fought back and eventually inflicted major losses. But their psychological effect was devastating.

For the prior six months, the president and his military leaders had been conducting a "Success Offensive," telling the American people that the U.S. was winning the War. No one could explain how an enemy that was supposedly beaten and ready for surrender could mount such a broad-based, well-coordinated series of attacks. Worse, the attacks went on for weeks. Some of the attacks, such as the highly symbolic one on the U.S. embassy in Saigon, were shown on U.S. television. The American public was outraged.

This proved the turning point in the War. In March 1968, amidst nationwide anti-War protests, a group of "Wise Men" that had been assembled to advise Johnson on the War recommended U.S. withdrawal. Johnson announced a temporary bombing halt and shocked the country with the announcement that he would not run for re-election in November. The Republican nominee, Richard Nixon, won the election, partly by promising that he had a plan to end the War and to achieve "peace with honor." He took office in January 1969.

## 1970 – 1973: De-escalation and Vietnamization

There were two elements to Nixon's concept of "peace with honor." First, any U.S. withdrawal must not betray even a hint of U.S. military defeat. Second, any withdrawal must provide at least a reasonable chance for the government of South Vietnam to survive on its own. Nixon's plan for achieving these objectives was called "Vietnamization."

Vietnamization meant shifting the burden of fighting from American forces to the South Vietnamese army. This required building up the strength of ARVN while steadily withdrawing U.S. troops. It also meant providing training, supplies and air cover to ARVN forces in the field as they learned to fight the War on their own. This would allow the U.S. to decrease its direct involvement in the

War while increasing the chances of survival of the government of South Vietnam.

In July 1969, the U.S. withdrew 25,000 troops from Vietnam. This was the first numerical reduction in forces since the escalation of advisers had begun in 1961. In March 1970, another 150,000 troops were withdrawn, and another 100,000 were removed at the end of 1971. By the beginning of 1972 only 175,000 U.S. troops remained in Vietnam.

As part of the material support for Vietnamization, in 1970 the U.S. transferred to ARVN: over 1,000,000 M-16 rifles; 12,000 M-60 machine guns; 40,000 M-79 grenade launchers; 2,000 heavy mortars and howitzers; and thousands of ships, airplanes, helicopters, tanks, and jeeps. So many airplanes were transferred that South Vietnam was left with the fourth largest air force in the world. The U.S. also invested in better training for ARVN forces and increased pay to reduce desertion rates by ARVN soldiers.

To lay the groundwork for successful hand over to ARVN, Nixon began a campaign of bombing Cambodia in March 1969. It was so secret that not even the Secretary of the Air Force was informed of it. The objective was to destroy military sanctuaries that were being used by the North to launch attacks on the South. In April 1970, Nixon authorized the ground invasion of Cambodia. When it was finally discovered and made public, the invasion produced an explosive reaction in the U.S. Over 500 college campuses erupted in protest. At Kent State in Ohio, peacefully protesting students were fired on from a distance by the Ohio National Guard. Four students were killed. This caused the protests to escalate even further.

The invasion produced limited military results. But it was a disaster for Nixon's strategy of staged withdrawal. Protests in the U.S. convinced the North that Nixon could not sustain the public support needed to continue the War. They recommitted to a defensive strategy of prolonging the War while minimizing their own casualties. They would wait the U.S. out, resisting U.S. proposals to end the War on U.S. terms. This defensive strategy changed in early 1972 when the North undertook one of the most important offensives of the entire War.

In March 1972, the U.S. had only 69,000 soldiers left in Vietnam and the North recognized the weakness of ARVN. On March 30th it began what became known as the Easter Offensive. It attacked the South along the DMZ in Quang Tri province, in the Central Highlands at Kontum, and in the southernmost part of the country, at An Loc. These attacks differed from prior initiatives in that they were a conventional offensive, supported by hundreds of Soviet- and Chinese-supplied tanks, heavy artillery, and anti-aircraft weapons. As with the earlier Tet Offensive, the Easter Offensive inflicted major psychological damage. Still worse, the North ended up controlling almost 10% of the territory in the South, including two provinces from which it could now launch sustained attacks from within the South.

The Easter Offensive greatly improved the North Vietnamese position. If Nixon's strategy to exit the War was to succeed he needed to change the faltering dynamic. So, he initiated a whole new level of air attacks against the North, declaring in private that he wanted to "level the goddamn country." Operation Linebacker targeted critical infrastructure in North Vietnam, including factories, power plants, rail depots, oil storage facilities, bridges connecting North Vietnam with China, and all of the country's major ports. North Vietnam, which had withdrawn from peace talks that were going on in Paris, came back to the bargaining table.

By January 1973, the U.S. and North Vietnam had reached an agreement to end the War. The basic terms of the agreement were as follows.

* The U.S. would withdraw its troops within 60 days.
* North Vietnamese troops would remain in the South.
* The North would return U.S. Prisoners Of War and assist in accounting for U.S. soldiers Missing In Action.
* A tripartite commission would be set up in the South. The existing U.S.-backed government, the Viet Cong, and the "neutralists" were the three parties.
* The U.S. would give North Vietnam $4.75 billion in economic aid to assist its rebuilding (this was never paid).

* It was acknowledged that the 17th parallel (from the 1954 Geneva Accords) was not a political or territorial division of the country.

President Thieu of South Vietnam protested the terms of the treaty and tried to sabotage it. But he was without options. President Nixon assured Thieu that the U.S. would continue to support South Vietnam with economic aid and offshore air support. The Paris Peace Accords were signed in January 1973 and on March 29, 1973, the last U.S. combat troops left Vietnam. Nixon, however, was forced from office in August 1974 for crimes he had committed (Watergate) trying to cover up his secret invasion of Cambodia. His commitment to Thieu, therefore, was never fulfilled.

## 1973 – 1975: Withdrawal and Collapse

Before leaving, the U.S. transferred title to all of its military installations to the government in the south. This was done to escape the peace treaty's prohibition against military support after U.S. withdrawal. President Thieu began a series of attacks against Viet Cong strongholds in the South. These were largely ineffectual. At the same time, the NVA and Viet Cong violated the Accords by stepping up their attacks on the South. U.S. bombing support for ARVN from offshore aircraft carriers was stopped in August 1973 when the Congress, in the Case-Church Amendment, cut off all funding for military activities in Vietnam. After more than two decades of continuous support, the U.S. had finally ended its military engagement in Vietnam.

By early 1974, the talks that were to form the new tripartite government had broken off. It didn't matter. With U.S. military and financial support removed, the economy in the South collapsed. At the same time, the North Vietnamese and the Viet Cong had begun plans for a final assault on Saigon, the South's capital. Morale among the South Vietnamese military was terrible, with almost 25% deserting in 1974. A heavy mood of defeatism lay over the country. The final fall came quickly.

In March 1975, the NVA attacked Hue and Da Nang, major cities on the central coast, and Kontum and Pleiku in the central highlands. The speed of their victory surprised everybody as the ARVN forces beat a furious retreat to the south. By April, the communists were on the outskirts of Saigon. With only a token defense, and only 55 days after the campaign had begun, Saigon fell to the communists. On April 30, 1975, the communists from the North raised their flag over the city. The War that had begun almost 30 years before was finally over.

# 3 Prominent Events and Themes

The choice of what to highlight in any major historical occurrence is somewhat arbitrary and somewhat self-fulfilling. In the case of the Vietnam War, the most important events were military and emerged from within Vietnam itself. But some important events were civilian and found their locus in the U.S. This, itself—the influence of U.S. civilians —is an intriguing phenomenon about the War, how it was fought, and why it was lost.

## Rolling Thunder

In early 1965, President Johnson authorized a series of bombing attacks on North Vietnam. Code named Rolling Thunder, they were intended to destroy the will and the capacity of the North to wage war. They were also meant to interdict supplies flowing from the North to the Viet Cong fighters in the South. The bombing targeted North Vietnamese ports, oil depots, ammunition dumps, roads, bridges, railways, power plants, and other civilian and industrial infrastructure as well as supply lines between the North and South.

By the time the War was over, the U.S. had dropped more than seven million tons of bombs. This was three times the total tonnage dropped in all theaters by all Allied forces during all of World War II combined. It amounted to 600 pounds of bombs for every man, woman and child in Vietnam. The bombing was killing over 1,000 civilians a week at its height and caused revulsion throughout the civilized world. Such figures did not deter some in the military from calling for even greater destruction. General Curtis LeMay, former Chief of Staff of the U.S. Air Force, stated in his 1965 biography that the U.S. "should bomb them back into the Stone Age."

The campaign did not meet its objectives. Supplies continued to flow south. And, far from breaking the will of the North to fight, it actually hardened its commitment to winning. Before Rolling Thunder, the War had been fought in the South, almost exclusively by local Viet Cong insurgents. The onset of bombing convinced the leadership of the North that it needed to take its War to the South in order to excise the source of the bombings. In other words, Rolling Thunder had the perverse effect of increasing the scale and intensity of the War in the South and accelerating the collapse of the U.S. position.

## Search and Destroy

The main ground-war tactic adopted by the U.S. military was called "Search and Destroy." It held that U.S. superiority in mobility, firepower and communications would allow it to achieve victory on the battlefield. U.S. Army Chief of Staff Harold K. Johnson wrote that the requirements for ground operations were, "Find the enemy; fix the enemy in place; fight and finish the enemy." This was right out of U.S. Army doctrine developed for a ground war against the Soviet Union in Europe. One campaign summary illustrates the nature of Search and Destroy.

Operation Jim Bowie in March 1966 involved six U.S. army battalions sent to flush out a reported Viet Cong stronghold in Binh Dinh province. Over the three weeks of the campaign, 30,000 helicopter sorties were flown. The Air Force dropped 215 tons of bombs and 102 tons of napalm. A total of 20,000 rounds of heavy artillery were fired, 95,000 gallons of fuel were used, and 626 tons of supplies were expended. A total of 27 Viet Cong fighters were killed, 17 were captured, and 19 weapons were recovered.

The effects of Search and Destroy on South Vietnamese civilians were devastating. U.S. troops moved from region to region, never getting to know the local people. The astounding amounts of firepower used wrought extraordinary damage. By the end of the War, more than 5 million civilians were killed, wounded or made refugees in their own country. More than 3,000 villages were damaged or destroyed, many intentionally. But despite such astonishing devastation, the U.S. never destroyed the enemy. Instead, its brutal tactics served frequently to recruit otherwise neutral Vietnamese to the enemy's side.

## Tet Offensive

On January 30th, 1968, the Viet Cong and the North Vietnamese Army launched a series of assaults aimed at breaking the back of the South Vietnamese Army. The "Tet Offensive" as it came to be known, radically changed the course of the War. It included attacks on over 100 hamlets, towns, and cities and dozens of military bases. Attackers even broke into the U.S. embassy compound in Saigon where they staged a five-hour fire fight with U.S. Marines. It was named "Tet" for the traditional Vietnamese Lunar New Year which was when it was launched. It caught both the U.S. and South Vietnamese military forces by surprise.

The attacks were eventually repulsed but their psychological effect was devastating. The reason is that for the prior six months, the Johnson administration had waged a public relations "Success Offensive" in the U.S., trying to shore up domestic support for the War. It promoted the idea that the U.S. was winning the War, and that, according to Robert McNamara, U.S. Secretary of Defense, "all available measures were showing progress." This myth was brutally exploded by the surprise, the breadth, the ferocity, and the tenacity of the fighting.

The administration and the military were seen as either deluded or deceitful in their representations to the American people. Walter Cronkite, America's most trusted newscaster, exploded on television, "I thought we were supposed to be winning this damn thing!" Tet proved the turning point in the War. Within weeks, plans had begun being drawn up for de-escalation and eventual withdrawal.

## Secret Bombing of Laos and Cambodia

From 1959 onward, North Vietnam funneled military aid to insurgents in the South. To do this, they used a series of roads and trails known as the Ho Chi Minh Trail. This north-south artery passed through the rugged, mountainous terrain of Laos and Cambodia, neutral countries that border Vietnam to the west. The North Vietnamese Army also used sanctuaries inside Laos and Cambodia to hide from U.S. and ARVN forces.

In 1962, the Kennedy administration began secretly bombing Laos. Its purpose was to cut off supplies moving along the Trail and to destroy enemy camps across the border in Laos. But Laos was a neutral country and the bombing violated international law as well as the Geneva Accords of 1954. By the time the bombing had ended in 1973, over 3,000,000 tons of bombs had been dropped, killing an estimated 350,000 Laotian civilians.

In March 1969, President Nixon began secretly bombing Cambodia. His purpose was to flush out NVA forces that were using the sanctuary of Cambodia to launch attacks into South Vietnam. The campaign lasted until 1973 during which time almost 400,000 tons of explosives were dropped. Civilian casualties from this bombing were estimated at between 500,000 and 600,000. Once exposed, the campaign incited massive worldwide protest. It also destroyed the social fabric of Cambodian society with the result that a communist group known as the Khmer Rouge seized power. Over the next five years it killed an estimated 1,700,000 Cambodian people.

## Persistent Lying to the American People

In 1971, classified documents relating to the War that had been smuggled from the Pentagon were published. The Pentagon Papers laid bare the fact that four successive administrations had lied repeatedly to the American public about the War in Vietnam. These lies concerned: 1) the true reason for the War; 2) the true nature of the War; 3) progress of the War; and, 4) the likelihood of its success.

The first set of lies concerned the true reason for the War. For years, the public rationale for U.S. involvement in Vietnam had been to keep Vietnam out of the hands of communists. But in March 1965, *before* the massive escalation that would make the War irreversible, a Pentagon briefing for the President stated that the true U.S. goals in Vietnam were:

"70% to avoid a humiliating U.S. defeat; 20% to keep South Vietnam (and adjacent territories) from Chinese hands; 10% to permit the people of Vietnam a better, freer way of life."

Had theses true priorities been made public, it is questionable whether the American people would have supported the War for as long as they did.

The second set of lies concerned the true nature of the War. Some U.S. programs, such as the CIA's Operation Phoenix, involved the "neutralization," i.e. assassination, of more than 20,000 civilian South Vietnamese believed to be collaborators of the Viet Cong. Mass murders by U.S. forces such as the massacre at My Lai where more than 500 civilians were intentionally killed, were much more common than officially admitted. The extension of the War through the illegal bombing of Laos and Cambodia was kept secret. U.S. ambassador to Laos, William Sullivan, wrote in this regard, "We can carry out these efforts only if we do not, *repeat do not*, talk about them, and when necessary, if we deny that they are taking place."

Third, both civilian and military officials routinely lied to Congress and the American people concerning the progress of the War. At every major escalation, in 1956, in 1961, and in 1965 internal appraisals of progress were dismal, even desperate. This differed greatly with the perennial optimism voiced to the public. The public was repeatedly told that the War was going fine, that the U.S. was winning, that there was "light at the end of the tunnel." U.S. Congressman Pete McCloskey summarized this practice of lying, saying that the Pentagon's "thousands of instances of deceit" with "hundreds of Congressmen" constituted "attempts to 'brainwash'" both the Congress and the American people.

The final set of lies involved the War's likelihood of success. From as early as the 1950s, *every* U.S. president privately expressed doubt about the prospect of the War ever being won at any acceptable cost. In January 1966, Secretary of Defense Robert McNamara told President Johnson that the U.S. had a one-out-of-three chance of winning on the battlefield. Johnson queried, "Then no matter what we do in the military field there is no sure victory?" McNamara's answer: "That's right." But Johnson, like Eisenhower and Kennedy before him, and Nixon after him, was captive to the ideology of anti-communism. None wanted to be the "first American president to lose a war." As a result, they chose to disguise the true likelihood of success and "soldier on."

## The First Televised War

Vietnam was the first televised war. World War II and the Korean War had both been filmed. To see footage, people had to go to movie theaters. Vietnam, however, was different. Not only was it captured in color, it was captured live and broadcast every night directly into the living rooms of millions of American households. The effect was stunning.

For the first time ever, the American public was shown—graphically—the true horrors of war. By the late 1960s televised footage of firefights, aerial bombings, use of napalm, and American soldiers fighting and dying in battle became an almost nightly occurrence. The immediacy of such images—and revulsion at the true picture of war that they provoked—helped turn many millions of Americans against the War.

As a result, the major news services that had initially supported the War came to be viewed by the military as virtual enemies. After Vietnam, the military learned to carefully manage journalists' access to and reporting on American wars. Witness, for example, the military's careful control of wartime reporting during the Iraq War through the use of "embedded" journalists. The result is a much more "sanitized" picture of war that is shown to the American people. It is one that sanctifies the military's objectives, idolizes its members, and aims to maintain support for military operations by the public back home.

## Massive Peace Protests at Home

The War provoked massive peace protests at home. In 1965, Alice Herz, a Jewish survivor of Nazi Germany, burned herself to death in Detroit to protest the War. Within months, 25,000 people protested the War in Washington D.C. By 1967, 50,000 protested, and by November 1969, 250,000 people assembled in Washington D.C. to protest the War. In May 1970, during a peaceful protest at Kent State University in Ohio, the Ohio National Guard shot from a distance and killed 4 students in an unarmed crowd. Within days, over 500 colleges and universities around the country had erupted in protest, not just of the War itself, but of the government's tactics to suppress dissent.

The protests involved the entire spectrum of the American public. Their role in either ending or prolonging the War is still hotly debated. On the one hand, their scope and intensity were major factors in the "Wise Men" telling President Johnson in March 1968 that he had to end the War. On the other hand, the protests almost certainly helped elect Richard Nixon president in 1969. While Johnson had signaled his effective abandonment of the War, Nixon prolonged it for another four years, intensifying the bombing and expanding the War into Cambodia.

Finally, the protests were closely watched by the leadership of North Vietnam who believed, correctly, that the U.S. could not sustain the War in the face of such massive internal dissent. On the basis of this, proponents of the War accused protesters of giving "aid and comfort to the enemy." This is a particularly provocative accusation since giving "aid and comfort to the enemy" is the definition of treason spelled out in the U.S. Constitution. Protest of government action is one the most sacred rights accorded Americans. It is the very mechanism by which the

United States came into existence. Its protection is enshrined in the First Amendment to the U.S. Constitution.

# 4  Why the U.S. Lost the War

The question of why the U.S. lost the Vietnam War is still hotly debated. It can be understood in terms of political failures, intelligence failures, and military failures. Within each of these three categories, we find three sub-categories of explanation.

## Political Failures

*The Essential Fiction of a "South" Vietnam.* Until the United States came in and set up an anti-communist military dictatorship, there had never been a "South" Vietnam. The U.S. created "South" Vietnam in order to avoid a communist victory in the Geneva-sponsored elections of 1956. The people of Vietnam knew nothing of the idea of two separate countries. For hundreds of years they had been a distinct people with a unique culture and a single language. Most Vietnamese didn't care whether they were governed by communists or capitalists as long as they were united as a single nation. Given this, the successive military regimes of the South could never gain a political consensus for a separate country.

Successive leaders who were given or seized power (Diem, Khanh, Ky, Thieu) simply carried out the political and military agenda they were hired by the United States to do. Thus it was that despite the expenditure of almost half a trillion dollars, two decades of fighting, the full weight of American prestige, and the deaths of over three million people, the fiction of a separate nation could not be sustained. Once U.S. props were removed, "South" Vietnam promptly disappeared.

*Unflagging Support for Illegitimate Regimes.* From the very beginning, U.S.-supported regimes lacked legitimacy. U.S. backing of the French was one key reason. Its undermining of the Geneva Accords was another. Still a third reason was that the leaders the U.S. installed in power were consistently alien and hostile to the people of Vietnam. Bao Dai is a conspicuous example. So, too, was Ngo Diem. Premier from 1955 until his assassination in 1963, Diem was a Catholic (a remnant of the French) in a nation of Buddhists. He was a Mandarin in a nation of peasants, an authoritarian in a nation of communitarian ethics. He was a northerner ruling in the south, a city-dweller in an agricultural nation, a wealthy man in a nation of intense poverty. In almost every possible way, he was alien to the people of Vietnam. And unlike Ho Chi Minh, the leader of the North who had actually fought the French for national liberation, Diem had not.

Worse, Diem's policies were corrupt and oppressive, especially toward the rural population.

While the North took land from wealthy landlords and gave it to peasants, Diem took land from peasants and gave it to his wealthy friends and family. Government jobs were routinely sold to the highest bidder with the understanding that the recipient could use the job to extort compensation from the people he oversaw. As resistance to Diem rose, civil rights were ruthlessly suppressed. Over 800,000 people were imprisoned and tens of thousands executed in an attempt to eradicate opposition. All of this bred deep enmity for Diem and the leaders who followed him. The Viet Cong and the North were successful in portraying leaders of the South as simply puppets of the Americans, propped up in an attempt to legitimize the foreigners' occupation of their country.

*American "Capture" by the Government of South Vietnam.* One of the bitter, infuriating ironies of Vietnam was that the more the U.S. committed to the War, the less leverage it had over its client in the South. Repeated South Vietnamese governments understood that having committed its reputation and international prestige, the U.S. could not leave. So, South Vietnamese regimes not only resisted U.S. pressure for reform, they were often actively defiant. The U.S. tried to get Diem, a Catholic, to stop persecuting Buddhist monks. Instead, he invaded Buddhist monasteries, setting off a huge conflagration of protest and oppression that brought condemnation from the entire world. The U.S. tried to weed out corruption. But corruption was the essential mechanism the government used to buy loyalty, so reforms were never made.

In many ways, then, the changes essential to building a stable, popular government, one with broad and enduring support among the people, were never implemented. The Americans were held hostage by their own very public commitment to military success. Without the means to improve the political situation, the U.S. was left with *only* military means to try to win the War. But since true victory meant creating a durable *political* entity, military means alone could never be enough.

## Intelligence Failures

*Confusion of Nationalism With Communism.* Vietnam was first and foremost a struggle for national independence. The Vietnamese people had thrown off the yoke of domination by the Chinese, the French and the Japanese. They were equally committed not to live under what they saw as simply another imperial power. It was this fervent nationalism, much more than any ideological embrace of communism, that motivated the Vietnamese to fight—and defeat—each of their successive invaders.

But the U.S. was fixated with containment and anti-communism. As noted above, it believed it had "lost" China in 1949. It had only fought Korea to a draw. In thrall to the domino theory, President Eisenhower declared that if the U.S. lost Vietnam it might lose all of Asia. By perceiving all global events through these lenses, U.S. leaders were unable to see the essentially nationalist character of the Vietnamese resistance. They were therefore unable to modify their strategies and tactics to accommodate the need for local self-determination. This proved a fatal blindness, contributing greatly to the ultimate loss of the War.

*Confusion of Partisan and Insurgency Warfare.* The U.S. concept of the War was that it was "partisan" rather than "insurgency" in nature, that it was being fought primarily by outside invaders—partisans—from the North. In fact, it was primarily an "insurgency" war being fought by locals in the South. This was certainly true at the time the U.S. began its massive escalation in 1965. The Viet Cong were partially supplied and reinforced by North Vietnam, but from the beginning, the primary source of opposition to U.S. regimes in the South arose from within the South itself. The misunderstanding of this fact greatly damaged U.S. efforts, since the strategy needed to fight one war was completely different from the strategy needed to fight the other.

The more the political situation deteriorated in the South, the more the U.S. bombed the North. The greater the Viet Cong hold on the rural population in the South, the more the U.S. bombed the North. The

U.S. was fighting a *military* campaign against invasion from the North when the real war was a *political* campaign between competing factions in the South. As noted above, this misunderstanding backfired on the U.S. because it drove the North to eventually (in mid-1968) enter the war in the South in strength in order to help expel the foreign occupiers who were attacking it from there.

*Poor Intelligence Going to Washington.* One of the most striking practices of the War was the falsification of intelligence reports sent to Washington. Everything from battle reports and field-level body counts, to situation assessments and reviews of strategic progress were routinely lied about. This made it impossible to perform meaningful assessments of the War's progress. Repeatedly, analysts who went to Vietnam and spent time *away* from the military came back with dramatically more pessimistic assessments of the War than those who simply relied on military information sources. The reason lay in the incentive structure of the military itself.

Military officers were rewarded for successful performance, not for failing performance. So, they had a built-in incentive to embellish the reports of their activities. Also, loyalty within the officer corps ensured that dissonant voices were punished with poor performance reviews, effectively ending their careers. Very quickly, then, the entire hierarchy of military reporting began creating false reports of progress. Once begun, the practice proved impossible to stop. Worse, it was impossible (until it was too late) to detect such lying and the rot that lay at its core.

## Military Failures

*Fundamental Failure of U.S. Military Strategy.* American firepower, mobility, and depth of resources were incalculably greater than those of its communist opponents. And, in fact, in most direct engagements between American and communist forces, the Americans were victorious, at least by the conventional definition of who remained on the battlefield at the end of the day. *Why, then, did America lose the War?* The answer is that the American military was beaten by a superior strategy. It was not so much out-fought as it was out-thought.

From the beginning of the escalation in 1965, the U.S. military chose a strategy of attrition. Attrition means that you progressively destroy the other side's forces until they can no longer fight. This was the essence of Napoleon's comment when asked before a battle which side God was on. Napoleon's reply: "God is on the side with the big battalions." But for attrition to work, three fundamental conditions must apply.

First, you must be able to control the timing and terms of engagement. Otherwise, you cannot ensure progressive destruction of the enemy's forces. Second, the enemy's losses must exceed his replacement rate. Otherwise, he can simply replace lost troops faster than they are being destroyed. And third, your own losses, while they may be far lower than those of the enemy, must still be tolerable within your own war-making context. Amazingly, none of these conditions applied. Even more amazing, even though they didn't apply, the American military never changed its fundamental strategy until it was too late.

A post-War review of thousands of engagements revealed that in almost 90% of the cases, firefights were engaged at the timing and in locations chosen by the enemy. Thus, if the U.S. could not control the timing or terms of engagement, attrition could not work. Second, intelligence estimates *during the War* indicated that some 200,000 North Vietnamese young men attained draft age every year. This was far higher than the rate at which they were being killed on the battlefield and still didn't consider Viet Cong recruiting in the south. Finally, despite killing more than nine enemy soldiers for every American lost, the costs to the U.S. became unbearable. As more and more U.S. soldiers came home in body bags, the American public turned against the War and demanded it be stopped.

Against the U.S. strategy of attrition, the North Vietnamese pursued a strategy of "enervation" or protracted war. This meant tiring the enemy of his will to fight. On the battlefield, enervation meant dragging out the War, harassing the enemy, avoiding serious engagement except where the likelihood of success was high, withdrawing before serious losses were sustained, and counting on the American public to tire of a seemingly endless but unwinnable war. This is the strategy Vietnam had used to defeat the French. It worked equally well to defeat the Americans.

*Failure of Interdiction.* Rolling Thunder, lasting from 1965 to 1968, was the principal instrument used by the U.S. to deter support by the North for the insurgency in the South. Its aim was to interdict supplies from the North so as to starve the War in the South. Interdiction failed for four reasons. First, the level of economic development of North Vietnam was very low, meaning there were few concentrations of useful targets to bomb. Second, when the air campaign began, the North dispersed even these targets throughout the countryside so as to protect them from bombing. Third, targets that were damaged were quickly rebuilt. For example, bridges over rivers were sometimes rebuilt nightly.

Fourth, and perhaps most important, since the War was primarily an "insurgency war," fought from within the South itself, the vast majority of the War's material requirements were provided locally. In 1965, the CIA reported that 31% of the weapons captured from the Viet Cong were of American manufacture. And at the height of the bombing in 1967, the CIA estimated that even if bombing intensity were *doubled*, it would still only interdict 20% of the supplies flowing south. In other words, bombing would have had to be increased *ten-fold* to completely shut off supplies from the North. This was not politically, economically, or even militarily possible.

*Ineffectiveness of ARVN.* One of the most frustrating aspects for the U.S. military in Vietnam was the ineffectiveness of the Army of the Republic of Vietnam. There were some notable, even heroic, exceptions, but from the earliest days, ARVN soldiers were reluctant or passive in the face of the enemy. Creighton Abrams, the U.S. General in charge at the time of the Easter Offensive, wrote of ARVN, "It is losing its will and cannot be depended upon to take the measures necessary to stand and fight." This is one of the reasons the U.S. concluded in 1965 that it would have to do the fighting itself. The reasons for this failure to fight effectively are three-fold.

First, many of the soldiers in the South Vietnamese Army were themselves either indifferent or even hostile to the U.S. mission in Vietnam. They saw the damage the War inflicted on their country and wanted the U.S. to leave. Second, because promotion was based not on experience, courage, or leadership but rather on loyalty and connections, the quality of the officer corps was exceptionally poor. Soldiers refused to put their lives at risk under the direction of inexperienced, cowardly, or corrupt officers. Finally, the whole of the army had been infiltrated by the Viet Cong. So, field maneuvers were routinely disclosed to the enemy before they ever began. This made it a near certainty that field operations would be ambushed, that fighting would be fierce, and that losses would be high. Knowing this, the U.S kept ARVN out of the loop of planning for many field operations. This was not a formula for effective collaboration or battlefield success.

# 5 Aftermath: The Loss of American Innocence

The Vietnam War changed the way the American people viewed themselves, at least for a while. As a result of the defeat, they experienced a dramatic decline in confidence in their governmental institutions. And the deception they learned that had been used to justify and prosecute the War led to a crisis of belief in authority. Finally, as a result of the way the War was fought, with massive bombings, chemical warfare, systematic killing of civilians, and vastly disproportionate force, they developed a more general aversion to the use of U.S. military power in other places in the world.

Part of the reason for these reactions was the belief Americans hold about how America came into the world. The narrative of America's founding is that at one time *it* was the small farming country on the fringe of civilization. *It* was the nation that had just wanted to be left alone to create its own destiny. *It* wanted an end to its own subjugation by the strongest imperial power in the world. The

American Revolution—the crucible in which the country was created—was about David and Goliath and self-determination versus rule from abroad. The Vietnam War turned that narrative on its head. In this way, the two wars—the American Revolutionary War and the Vietnam War—were eerily similar, though reverse images of each other.

## Similarities Between the American Revolutionary and Vietnam Wars

The Colonies won the Revolutionary War but it was one of the most improbable victories in history. They were largely a bunch of volunteers on the fringes of civilization, fighting against the greatest military power in the history of the world. The Vietnam War was the same, only now it was the Vietnamese as underdogs and the U.S. as foreign military occupier. How did they win?

Now it was America that was the mightiest power on earth while Vietnam was the small nation of farmers on the other side of the world. It was American weapons and American soldiers that killed millions of Vietnamese to impose a political system that they did not understand and did not want. It was American money that was being used to prop up a corrupt, alien government against the wishes of its own people. And it was precisely the knowledge of this role reversal that made it so difficult for Americans to come to terms with their country's behavior in the War. In 1978, 71% of Americans

| Colonists versus the British | Vietnamese versus the Americans |
|---|---|
| The Colonists fought a "People's War" against the "conventional war" of the British. They stayed dispersed and fought opportunistically, only when they had a high chance of winning. | The Vietnamese fought a "People's War" against the "conventional war" of the Americans. They stayed dispersed and fought opportunistically, only when they had a high chance of winning. |
| The Colonists yielded the cities to the British but kept control of the countryside where they could move about easily and live off the land. | The Vietnamese yielded the cities to the Americans but kept control of the countryside where they could move about easily and live off the land. |
| The Colonists focused mainly on the political war—winning the hearts and minds of the American people. The military war was always secondary to the political war. | The Vietnamese focused mainly on the political war—winning the hearts and minds of the Vietnamese people. The military war was always secondary to the political war. |
| The Colonists were fighting on their own soil, for the country of their forefathers, against an occupying army of foreign mercenaries. | The Vietnamese were fighting on their own soil, for the country of their forefathers, against an occupying army of foreign mercenaries. |
| The Colonists were fighting for a noble ideal: freedom from centuries of colonial domination. | The Vietnamese were fighting for a noble ideal: freedom from centuries of colonial domination. |
| The Colonists were assisted in the war by the two arch-enemies of the British: the French and the Spanish. | The Vietnamese were assisted in the war by the two arch-enemies of the Americans: the Russians and the Chinese. |
| The Colonists had nowhere else to go but they knew the patience of the British people would eventually run out. | The Vietnamese had nowhere else to go but they knew the patience of the American people would eventually run out. |

believed that Vietnam had been a mistake. A full 59% expressed the conviction that the War had been immoral. This would leave a cloud of doubt about American motives and American "exceptionalism" for many years to come.

## The Vietnam Syndrome.

For years, the explicit public objective of the U.S. in Vietnam had been to prevent the country from falling into the hands of a communist government. But that is exactly what happened. The U.S. lost the War. Worse, Vietnam was the *first* war America had ever lost. The cost to the U.S. self-image of invincibility was extraordinarily high. Within a few years of the U.S. withdrawal, then-former President Nixon spoke of a "Vietnam Syndrome" that had come to afflict the country.

The Vietnam Syndrome referred to the aversion to the use of military force in pursuing U.S. foreign policy objectives. More specifically, it pointed to an unwillingness on the part of the public to accept the loss of American lives in foreign entanglements. The U.S. quickly pulled out of Lebanon in 1982 when 240 Marines were killed in a barracks bombing. It quickly left Somalia in 1993 after 18 soldiers were killed in a battle in Mogadishu. (This was the basis of the popular movie, *Black Hawk Down.*) The American public would not tolerate the large loss of American lives in foreign wars the way they had accepted losses in World War II and Korea.

So, America's new wars were redesigned to avoid battlefield combat whenever possible. Witness the emergence of high technology "wars at a distance," such as the First Gulf War against Iraq, from 1990 – 1991, where there were fewer than 100 American deaths, or the War in Kosovo in 1998 – 1999 where there was not even *one* American killed.

The changes to U.S. policy as a result of Vietnam initially suggested that military force should be used only when critical national interests are at risk. It should be used only as a last resort and only when there is substantial public backing for its use. Once committed, the military should be allowed to use whatever resources are needed to win. It should never be used unless there are clear objectives and an explicit definition of victory. And finally, there should be a clearly defined exit strategy. These guidelines are known as the "Powell Doctrine." They were articulated by Gen. Colin Powell, Chairman of the Joint Chiefs of Staff and later Secretary of State, who had served as an army officer in Vietnam.

It was expected that these guidelines would help prevent the entanglement of the U.S. into future Vietnams, quagmires that sapped the American spirit and hampered the implementation of U.S foreign policy. But in 1991, following the first Gulf War, President George H. W. Bush declared, "Thank God we've finally beaten the Vietnam Syndrome." Recent U.S. military attacks in Afghanistan, Pakistan, Iraq, Yemen, Somalia, and Libya suggest that that statement may, in fact, be true: that the experience of Vietnam no longer deters easy recourse to military force. At the very least, the new use of drones to kill without ever engaging soldiers on the ground, suggests that even if the Vietnam Syndrome has not been beaten, it has been bypassed via a technological workaround.

# 6 Final Word

Vietnam was an incredibly damaging exercise in the use of military force for achieving what could not be achieved diplomatically. It cost the lives of 58,000 American soldiers and an estimated 3 million southeast Asians. In economic terms, it cost almost half a trillion dollars and grievously damaged the economy of the United States. Perhaps the greatest damage was to the moral stature and the reputation of the U.S. in the world.

Vietnam had never attacked the U.S., had never threatened to attack, had no desire to attack, and had no capacity to attack. Instead, it had come to the U.S. for help in freeing itself from the same kind of colonial domination that the U.S. had freed itself from in its own Revolutionary War. But rather than helping the Vietnamese, the U.S. assumed the role of the adversary, first helping the French, and then fighting the Vietnamese directly to prevent them from achieving their own national independence and consent of the governed.

The two intellectual architects of the U.S. role in Vietnam were George F. Kennan and Robert S. McNamara. Kennan had devised Containment, the post-World War II strategy that defined U.S. actions vis-à-vis the Soviet Union in the Cold War. McNamara was U.S. Secretary of Defense from 1961 to 1968, first under President Kennedy and then under President Johnson. He is the unquestioned architect of the U.S. role in the War.

In 1980, Kennan described Vietnam as "the most disastrous of all of America's undertakings over the whole two hundred years of its history." In 1995, McNamara published his reflections and memoirs of his experience titled, *In Retrospect: The Tragedy and Lessons of Vietnam*. In it, he wrote, "We of the Kennedy and Johnson administrations who participated in the decisions on Vietnam acted according to what we thought were the principles and traditions of this nation. We made our decisions in light of those values. Yet we were wrong, terribly wrong. We owe it to future generations to explain why."

# 7 Timeline

| | | |
|---|---|---|
| 1946 | | Vietnam requests U.S. help evicting French colonialists. U.S. helps French instead. |
| 1950 | | Truman sends first U.S. military advisers to Vietnam. |
| 1954 | *May* | French defeated at Dien Bien Phu. U.S. takes over. |
| | *July* | Geneva Accords specify national elections, removal of foreign troops. |
| 1955 | | U.S. installs Ngo Diem as president of the new "South" Vietnam. |
| 1956 | | Eisenhower presses Diem to boycott Geneva-sponsored national elections. |
| 1960 | | National Liberation Front (Viet Cong) formed to create insurgency in south. |

| 1962 | American military advisers in Vietnam reach 12,000 in number. | |
|------|---------|----------|
| 1963 | *Nov. 1* | CIA-backed coup overthrows South Vietnamese President Diem. |
| | *Nov. 22* | Kennedy is assassinated. Johnson assumes Presidency. |
| 1964 | Gulf of Tonkin Resolution gives President essentially unlimited war powers. | |
| 1965 | *March* | U.S. begins Rolling Thunder, sustained bombing of North Vietnam. |
| | | First U.S. ground combat troops arrive in Vietnam. |
| | *November* | Ia Drang—first large-scale battle between U.S. and North Vietnamese troops. |
| 1967 | Half a million U.S. combat forces are on the ground in Vietnam. | |
| 1968 | *January* | Tet Offensive: massive attacks on U.S. facilities throughout Vietnam. |
| | *February* | Secretary of Defense Robert McNamara, chief architect of the War, resigns. |

| | *March* | President Johnson declares he will not seek re-election. |
| 1969 | *March* | Nixon begins secret bombing of Cambodia. |
| | *June* | U.S. withdraws 25,000 troops, first reduction since escalation began in 1961. |
| 1970 | *April* | U.S. invades Cambodia. |
| | *May* | Anti-War protests at over 500 U.S. colleges. Students killed at Kent State. |
| | *June* | Congress rescinds 1964 Gulf of Tonkin Resolution. |
| 1971 | | Pentagon Papers published. Massive government lying regarding Vietnam exposed. |
| 1972 | *May* | Nixon orders mining of North Vietnamese harbors, bombing of Hanoi. |
| | *December* | Christmas bombings—round-the-clock B52 raids on Hanoi. |
| 1973 | *January* | Paris Peace Accords signed. U.S. agrees to withdraw from Vietnam. |

| | | |
|---|---|---|
| | *March* | Last U.S. military forces leave Vietnam. |
| | *August* | Last U.S. bombing campaign in Southeast Asian War— over Laos. |
| 1975 | *April* | Communist forces capture Saigon. Fall of South Vietnam. |

If you enjoyed this book, please look for all of the titles in *The Best One-Hour History* series.

- Ancient Greece
- Rome
- The Middle Ages
- The Renaissance
- The Protestant Reformation
- European Wars of Religion
- The English Civil Wars
- The Scientific Revolution
- The Enlightenment
- The American Revolution
- The French Revolution
- The Industrial Revolution
- Europe in the 1800s
- The American Civil War
- European Imperialism
- World War I
- The Interwar Years
- World War II
- The Cold War
- The Vietnam War

To learn more about each title and its expected publication date, visit: *http://onehourhistory.com*

Made in the USA
San Bernardino, CA
16 March 2016